Dear Parent:

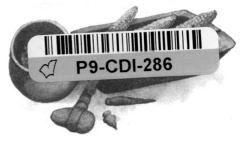

Congratulations! Your child is taking the first steps on an exciting journey. The destination? Independent reading!

STEP INTO READING® will help your child get there. The program offers five steps to reading success. Each step includes fun stories and colorful art. There are also Step into Reading Sticker Books, Step into Reading Math Readers, Step into Reading Write-In Readers, Step into Reading Phonics Readers, and Step into Reading Phonics First Steps! Boxed Sets—a complete literacy program with something for every child.

Learning to Read, Step by Step!

Ready to Read Preschool–Kindergarten
• big type and easy words • rhyme and rhythm • picture clues
For children who know the alphabet and are eager to begin reading.

Reading with Help Preschool–Grade 1
• basic vocabulary • short sentences • simple stories
For children who recognize familiar words and sound out new words with help.

Reading on Your Own Grades 1–3
• engaging characters • easy-to-follow plots • popular topics
For children who are ready to read on their own.

Reading Paragraphs Grades 2–3
• challenging vocabulary • short paragraphs • exciting stories
For newly independent readers who read simple sentences with confidence.

Ready for Chapters Grades 2–4
• chapters • longer paragraphs • full-color art
For children who want to take the plunge into chapter books but still like colorful pictures.

STEP INTO READING® is designed to give every child a successful reading experience. The grade levels are only guides. Children can progress through the steps at their own speed, developing confidence in their reading, no matter what their grade.

Remember, a lifetime love of reading starts with a single step!

To Marsha Mirsky

Text copyright © 1994 by Lucille Recht Penner.
Illustrations copyright © 1994 by Pamela Johnson.
All rights reserved under International and Pan-American Copyright Conventions.
Published in the United States by Random House Children's Books, a division of
Random House, Inc., New York, and simultaneously in Canada by Random House
of Canada Limited, Toronto.

www.stepintoreading.com

Educators and librarians, for a variety of teaching tools, visit us at
www.randomhouse.com/teachers

Library of Congress Cataloging-in-Publication Data
Penner, Lucille Recht.
The true story of Pocahontas / by Lucille Recht Penner ; illustrated by Pamela Johnson.
    p.   cm. — (Step into reading. A step 3 book)
SUMMARY: An introduction to the life of Pocahontas, a seventeenth-century Powhatan Indian
known for befriending Captain John Smith and the English settlers of Jamestown.
ISBN 0-679-86166-1 (trade) — ISBN 0-679-96166-6 (lib. bdg.)
1. Pocahontas, d. 1617—Juvenile literature.   2. Powhatan women—Biography—Juvenile
literature.   3. Powhatan Indians—Biography—Juvenile literature.   [1. Pocahontas, d. 1617.
2. Powhatan Indians—Biography.   3. Indians of North America—Biography.
4. Women—Biography.]   I. Johnson, Pamela, ill.   II. Title.   III. Series: Step into reading.
Step 3 book.   E99.P85   P5755   2003   975.5'01'092—dc21   2002014526

Printed in the United States of America   37 36 35 34 33 32 31 30 29 28

STEP INTO READING, RANDOM HOUSE, and the Random House colophon are registered
trademarks of Random House, Inc.

STEP INTO READING®

STEP 3

The True Story of
Pocahontas

by Lucille Recht Penner
illustrated by Pamela Johnson

Random House 🏠 New York

Pocahontas is the daughter
of the great Chief Powhatan.
Her name means "playful one."

Her people are the Powhatans.
They live in houses
made of saplings,
and pray to their gods.

Pocahontas has a secret name, too.
It is Little Snow Feather.

Her father has many wives
and more than a hundred children.
Pocahontas is his favorite.
She loves to play
with her sisters and brothers.

When Pocahontas is ten years old,

three English ships appear.

The Powhatans have never

seen anything like them.

They call the ships "floating islands."

What are they doing here?

Men get off the ships.

How strange they look!

They have hair on their faces.

The newcomers wear strange clothes.

Pocahontas and her friends giggle.

They call the strangers

"coat-wearing people."

The Englishmen begin
chopping down trees.
They build a fort, a church,
and little houses.
They call their new town
Jamestown.

One man points a big stick.

Boom! Boom!

Smoke and fire shoot out.

A bird falls down dead.

Is this magic?

Some Powhatans trade corn
to the strangers.
They get pretty glass beads,
bells, and little mirrors.

Others don't like the strangers.

They shoot arrows at them.

Soon the Englishmen are afraid

to leave their fort.

They can't hunt or fish.

Their food is almost gone.

Captain John Smith is

a leader of the Englishmen.

He goes hunting for food.

A Powhatan is his guide.

Suddenly arrows fly through the air.

Captain Smith holds his guide

in front of him as a shield.

He whips out his pistol.

But he stumbles and falls

into an icy swamp.

There is no escape.

The Powhatans pull him out.

They rub his freezing legs.

Then they take him to

Chief Powhatan.

A great shout goes up
when Captain Smith enters
the Chief's house.

Pocahontas's aunt,

Queen Oppussoquionuske

(Oh-puss-so-kee-on-us-kee),

brings him water to wash his hands

and a great bunch of feathers to dry them.

A feast is served.

Everyone eats roasted deer meat,

bread, corn, and turkey.

Then Chief Powhatan gives a signal.

Men grab Captain Smith.

They push him down

and raise their heavy clubs.

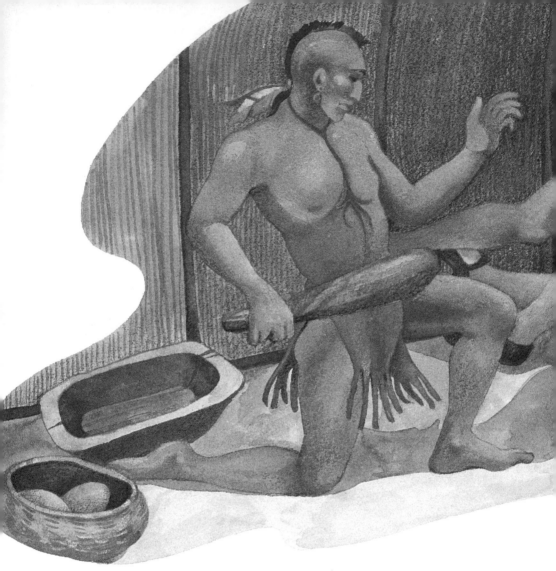

But suddenly Pocahontas

rushes forward.

She runs in front of the warriors

and throws her arms

around Captain Smith's head.

The chief cries out
and the warriors fall back.
Pocahontas has saved the life
of Captain John Smith!

Now John Smith and Pocahontas
are good friends.

She visits him at Jamestown.

She helps the hungry English people

trade with the Powhatans

for corn and meat.

Pocahontas races and plays games

with the English children.

She learns to turn somersaults.

It's fun!

She turns over and over.

Pocahontas wants to talk
to her English friends.
She uses sign language.
When she puts her hand
over her heart, it means
"I am your friend."

But not all the Powhatans
are friends with the Englishmen.
One day Captain Smith is
in another fight.
He captures seven Powhatans
and takes them to Jamestown.

Chief Powhatan sends Pocahontas

to ask for his men back.

Pocahontas has been a good friend

to the English people.

Without her help they might

have starved.

Captain Smith says,

"I will let them go

for your sake."

One day Captain Smith and his men
go to visit Chief Powhatan.
The Chief is not home.
While they wait,
Pocahontas and her friends
sing and dance for them.

When the Chief returns,

Captain Smith tells him that King James

has sent him presents.

They are waiting in Jamestown.

"Bring them here to me,"

Chief Powhatan says.

"I am a king too!"

King James has sent the Chief

a copper crown,

rings for his fingers,

a bright red cloak,

a basin and pitcher,

and a big bed with a canopy.

It is hard work to

drag the presents through the woods.

The Chief puts on the red cloak.

He sits on the bed.

In return, he gives the Englishman

his deerskin cloak, his moccasins,

and some baskets of corn.

Later, Captain Smith goes exploring
in his canoe.
A spark falls
on the gunpowder box
he wears around his waist.
It bursts into flames.
Captain Smith is badly burned.
He goes home to England.

After Captain Smith leaves,
the Englishmen and the Powhatans
fight more and more often.

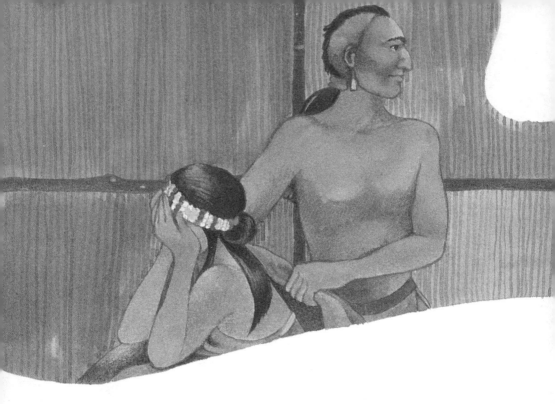

Samuel Argall is the captain
of an English ship.
He makes a plan
to capture Pocahontas.
That will force her father
to make peace.
Captain Argall asks his friend
Jopassus to help him.
In exchange, he will give Jopassus
a copper kettle.

Pocahontas is visiting Jopassus
and his wife.
Jopassus's wife pretends
she wants to visit an English ship.
Jopassus says she may go only
if Pocahontas goes too.
Pocahontas does not want to go.
But Jopassus's wife cries,
so Pocahontas agrees.

Captain Argall serves them dinner
in his cabin.

Everyone eats and drinks and smiles.

But when the meal is over,

the Captain says Pocahontas

is his prisoner.

She is very frightened,

but she does not cry.

Jopassus and his wife
get into their canoe
with the copper kettle.
They pretend to cry because Pocahontas
has been captured.

Captain Argall sends a message
to Chief Powhatan:
"We have your daughter.
We will not give her back
unless you make peace
and send us some corn."

Chief Powhatan wants his daughter,
but he is very angry
at the Englishmen.
He doesn't do what they ask.

Captain Argall is worried
because Pocahontas is so quiet and sad.
He tells her she will be treated
like a princess.
Then he takes her to a house
where the people are kind to her.
They give her English clothes to wear
and new leather shoes.

She eats with

a knife and spoon.

She learns to say grace

before she eats.

Pocahontas becomes a Christian.

She is given a new name: Rebecca.

A young man comes

to visit Pocahontas.

His name is John Rolfe.

John is a tobacco planter.

Pocahontas shows him

how her people plant tobacco.

They talk together.

John and Pocahontas

like each other very much.

He asks her to marry him,

and she says, "Yes."

The wedding is in a little church
in Jamestown.
The church is decorated
with bright wildflowers.
Pocahontas wears
a beautiful dress from England.

Pocahontas and John have a baby.
They name him Thomas.
They decide to take him
to visit England.

Chief Powhatan sends his friend
Tomocomo with them.
He gives Tomocomo a stick.
"Notch the stick," he says,
"each time you see an Englishman.
I want to know how many there are."

When the boat lands,

Tomocomo sees thousands of people.

He throws away the stick.

There are too many people

to count.

Where is the sky?

Where are the trees?

At home Pocahontas could

see for miles.

But here the air

is dark and smoky.

The streets are full

of tall stone houses.

It's hard to find
a way between them.
People ride around
in little houses on wheels.
Pocahontas is glad to ride, too.
The hard cobblestones
hurt her feet.
At home she could
walk miles on the
soft green earth.

She looks out.

There is so much to see!

Workmen pull carts

loaded with wood and bricks.

Women are selling cakes,

flowers, and even fish.

"Buy mine!" they shout.

Captain John Smith

comes to visit Pocahontas.

She has not seen him

for eight years.

They talk and talk.

Pocahontas goes to many parties.

The women dress in silk and satin.

Men wear tall hats
with curling feathers.

They think all Indians are savages,

but Pocahontas acts like a princess.

She stands very straight.

She smiles and speaks softly.

How pretty she is!